Secret Society

Sarah Plumb

Presentation by *BookLeaf Publishing*

Web: www.bookleafpub.com

E-mail: info@bookleafpub.com

ISBN: 9789358310351

First edition 2023

To Maia, the most interesting human I know

ACKNOWLEDGEMENT

Thank you to all the students who made me a better writer and a better person.

Secret Society

I belong to a secret society
Of 12 year olds trapped inside the bodies of
middle-aged
Falling-apart people
Confident now, in their particular brand of 12
year old strange
We like blob tag and pop tarts
We eat cake for breakfast and light things on fire
whenever we can
Cry along with animated movies
Sing ridiculous, made-up songs in the shower,
and obsess about the person
We want to like us

It's a small group
But, I wonder
If everyone secretly wants to join

Sky Child

There are those who encourage you to fly
By clipping your wings.

But, the moon still breaks through
the naked branches in the spring
no matter how ragged your wings are,

reaches out to me behind glass and pulls on the
ocean inside, reminding me where and to whom
I belong:
a sky child,
the flicker of an ember riding the wind.
With no wings at all, I take flight
and rise into the star filled night.

Appointed the Protector of Wishes

Pandora's impulse control has nothing on me.

Protector of wishes?
That was not a job I signed up for,
Certainly not one I am qualified to do.

The racers in my head carry on a spirited
dialogue.
Just one.
Don't touch that bottle, Sarah.
Maybe it's not even a good wish.
Sometimes people would do better if they didn't
get the stupid things they wish for.

The rule follower, afraid to disappoint, bites
back.
How would you even know? That's asinine.
Don't touch it. Just look at it. Practice your
breathing, for God's sake. You don't get to
decide.
But, the impulsive Sarah was never one to be
ignored.

I think to myself that a good wish would be
warm,

and my hand has a life of its own
impelling me to touch,
to know the smoothness of the glass
to feel the heat
Just to see.

Maybe if I can just get close enough to the glass,
I can see the wish
twinkling behind Coke bottle glasses
Magnified

And that way, maybe I won't have to open it at
all
because I'll know,

And somehow, I always have to know.
I reach out.

Toad

I used to walk fast
but, at 45,
I have joined the wanderers
inching along the pine needle carpet at a snail's
pace
on broken knees and an aching back.

Hello, Spidey, I say to the tiny creature hiding so
efficiently in the crack of the siding.
I pause to trade secrets with the baby finch
panting in her bed of grass under the eave.
And marvel at the bees taking a sip of water,
their mouths unfurling,
a little built in straw.

And I am thankful for this pain
that connects me to the Grasshopper,
to the Ant in the folds of the peony
to the Bunny

hidden in the undergrowth, chewing clover
and gives me time to be friends with the baby
Toad, barely visible against the soil,
climbing mountains of grass.

Vertigo

Last year, I had terrible vertigo
The world spun with every movement of my
head
I spent eight weeks motion sick
Smashing into walls, puking on the side of the
road

It is frightening when the world spins faster than
your eyes

Antibiotics let my eyes and ears connect
but I am still untethered
chasing spinning thoughts that refuse to be
caught
disconnected from coherence

Am I thinking nothing or everything?
I wonder if I'm getting dumber
conversations where words keep just out of
reach,
I don't know how to tell you;
the place where my thoughts meet my tongue is
lost.

With his head on my knee, I can be brave.

He looks at me;
one eye smaller than the other with a mop of
hair in his face.
His warm fur under my fingertips, the trees stop
spinning.

Bodhi, I say,
Let's go home.

Birkenstocks

When you slip on someone's well worn
Birkenstocks
Note the instep
The toes
The way the arch doesn't quite line up

The step isn't right.
Feet twinge,
You tire more quickly
The thought of a day in them
Trying to meld them to your feet, or your feet
To them
Isn't comfortable

My life takes place in Birkenstocks that
are not mine.
Each step out of place.
I simply do not fit.

Homebody

In another life,
I was a freight hopper
or perhaps I worked for a trader, or in shipping,
in a camel caravan,
or a voyageur smoking his pipe to the reflection
of the trees on the water

All I know is that I have a wandering soul
a homebody with deep roots
driven to escape, if only
to come home again

I want to get in my car and drive
until I no longer feel the bees buzzing deep in
my brain
a pressure cooker in my chest
to escape into something new
to reinvent myself

But, I always turn back, for fear
of letting you down.

Sunrise

There is a moment when the pale orb of the
moon
gives way
and the lake burns with orange,
its breath reaching out to the warmth of the day,
when the robin who can't yet be seen calls out to
the world,
announcing the permanence of his being

A grebe, I think,
makes a rush from the shore as we approach
and I murmur, one scared being to another,
I won't hurt you.

It is in that moment that I feel most genuinely
human,
my footsteps in line with the click of my dog's
paws,
believing that the dawn
makes my babble intelligible to ducks
and other critters.

Beautiful

It is not the curve of your lips or the smoothness
of your skin
It is not the coloring of your eyes
But the light in them
As you seek the sunrise
Over the forest

Sunset

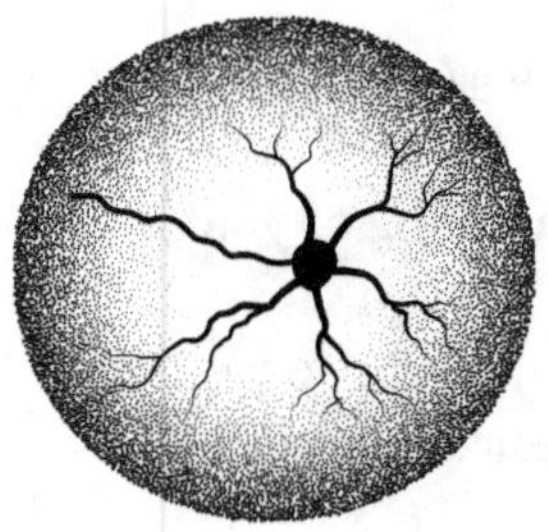

In the lap of water shaking hands with the dock
a hazy sun descending orange
in the west
The cattails comb the wind

The atoms of the sand between and the toes
within
long to hold one another again,
meld into a nebula of the early solar system

Blob shaped cells held beneath my skull wonder
how 'alive' and 'not,'
created from the same gaseous beginning,
can be so different?
If they are at all.
Or, maybe the sand,
awake,
rolling over in her lake bed,

ponders the same,
Wonders how I survive
my transience
and how our atoms
share the space
but never really touch.

Bryan Reynolds - Definitely Not for Everyone ™

An acquaintance friend of mine connected with
me on LinkedIn
and I laughed when I saw his tagline:
Definitely Not For Everyone ™

But, in the weeks since,
I find myself thinking of it often

Remembering how he showed up with boots for
the kid who had none,
with tools when fences fell apart,
and with healing words when hearts did.

I want to live in a world where no one might
ever believe

they could not be for everyone,
a world that honors humanity
honesty
generosity, and
kindness
over influencers and make-up moguls
a world where the tagline reads,
'Bryan Reynolds -
Appreciated by Everyone.'

The Storm

Before we were domesticated,
The wild existed beneath our naked skin

The warm animal in me,
Bored,
Hibernating,
warily watching for freedom
from behind the cage of underwire and mascara,
suburban malls and air conditioning

On a hot, muggy day,
When the temperature drops ten degrees in 6
minutes with the pressure
The drone of traffic covered by the whipping
wind
Branches swaying in a churning envelope above
the land
The woods, silent
Just the dog and I, and the wind
Distant grumbles and crashing thunder
Flashes
The splat of fat raindrops against the fat clover

I stand, arms extended
A witch

Wild
Every cell of my body alive
I believe
For a moment
That I am the lightning
Wildness and fury coursing within

Spent, the wind drops.
We climb to the car,
settling to domestication
again.

Sarah-speak

There is a language people speak,
called "Sarah."
Only a few follow the twists and turns,
half sentences,
giant leaps from one thought to another
mid-sentence, unexplained,
the words I can't find in memory replaced with
beeps or hand gestures,
alleys and raspberry bush tunnels I crawl
through to make myself known

13 year olds are natural Sarah-speakers,
but most adults seem to have lost the ability to
communicate
in my natural tongue -
a huge, wide, cultural gulf between us -
which is why
we don't get along.

We can only point and gesture at one another
in English.

How can I tell you the rush
if you have never felt it -
the relief -
when we find one another,
the Sarah-speakers and I?

The Writer

Coming along in the 11th hour
to save the world
as it once was
from being forgotten
to introduce the world to figments of invisible
imagination

Hemingways of 5000 years ago never stood a
chance
They are dust
gone
into the ephemeral space between nothing and
no one

Does it matter that my fingers rebel against the
force of holding an instrument that was never
meant to be there?

Zoom

There is a robin
defending his nest,
bashing his head again and again against a
window
His reflection
the enemy.

I know how he feels.
It's my reaction, too,
when I see my double chin in the Zoom window
when I see my photo
I, too, want to bash my head into the glass,
an enemy that exists only in my head.

An owl swoops low
hooting at me
disturbed by my footsteps and the playful jaunt
of my dog
under her roost.

I know, I say.
I, too, wish to go back to the time
before someone invaded my peace.

Top 5

This morning, I ranked the people
that I love
in terms of the ferocity
in which I love them.
I don't know what caused me to think this,
or why
I entertained the thought,
but, two dogs
ranked in the top 5.

Magenta

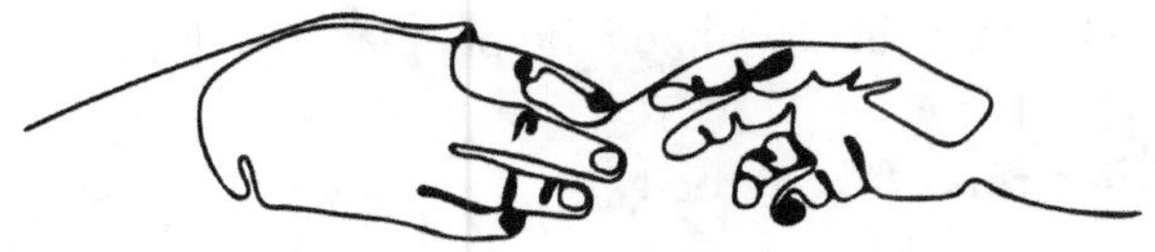

Do you ever think about how weird it is that we
have hair,
fused together,
growing out of the tips of our fingers?
And then, if that wasn't weird enough,
we paint it red, or cherry pink.

Loud fingers,
making a statement
but I'm not sure what it is

I just know that when my fingernails were
painted magenta
I could think of nothing else
except getting it off.
Every time the color flashed in the corner of my
eye
I would wince,
ball my hands into fists to try to
force the brutal color from my body.

And when I finally went and paid a ridiculous
sum of money
for a stranger to grind it off my fingers,
I couldn't stop smiling.

Barred Owl

In the saddle of two hills
Violet shadowed trees look down upon me,
my arms around cottonwood,
stretched nearly straight against the
circumference.
Deep grooves echo, hollow against the brush of
my face.
A single frog thrills.
I am being watched.

The dog,
his mind busy with the smells of plants and
bunnies
has failed to notice.

The Barred Owl blinks amber eyes
on a branch just ahead
she is waiting,
hoping that I will disturb her dinner,
me a spaniel, flushing

I am glad to be of use
but have no particular skill in finding game
just the usual clumsiness
inherent in humanity.

So, instead, we watch one another,
each of us weighing the other's role in our lives.

Words

Spelling isn't always my friend
But the play of words on my tongue is
The way they feel to use
Glitter in conversation
Lines of geese on a page

Outlaws

For a while, I wondered how other people made
friends so easily.
I wanted to be seen and wanted
but somehow, I never was invited to go or be or
do.

I often wonder who will attend my funeral.
I think,
when I die,
most people will have other plans:
an important meeting,
a haircut,
or be on vacation.

As I think these things, I find myself ramping up
into a meltdown.
(1 part frustration, 1 part boredom, 2 parts pain,
and 5 parts overwhelm.)
I voice aloud,
How did you never see this in yourself?
And talk myself through what I now recognize.

But, how can I ever be lonely with a tribe of
misfits?
The outlaws,

those of us who never really fit but somehow find one another.